ANIMAL COMPANIONS:

Your Friends, Teachers & Guides

Written by
DIANE POMERANCE, Ph.D.

Illustrated by
VANESSA MIER

POLAIRE PUBLICATIONS
Flower Mound, Texas

Printed in the United States of America
First Printing: 2003

06   05   04   03 010   1 2 3 4 5

Cover and text illustrations by Vanessa Mier
Book design by Diane Pomerance, Ph.D.
and Crystal Wood, Tattersall Publishing, Denton, Texas

For information, write to:
Polaire Publications
PMB 217
2221 Old Justin Rd., Ste. 119
Flower Mound, Texas 75028

www.animalcompanionsandtheirpeople.com

ISBN 0-9708500-2-6

DEDICATION

This book is dedicated to my beautiful and beloved canine family members who have brought me such profound joy, peace, comfort and love and who have truly served as my friends, teachers and guides. I cannot imagine life without the loyal, unconditionally loving presence of Katie, Caesar, Spencer and Sophie. It is they who have engendered my love and admiration of, and respect and appreciation for all animals. It is they who have inspired this book.

In particular, this book is dedicated to my beloved German Shepherd, Kaitlyn Cybill Shepherd, who was my first "big dog," who served as the matriarch of eleven other dogs, and who was the finest and dearest friend one could ever hope to have. I miss her radiant, brilliant, uncannily telepathic and charismatic presence each and every day of my life.

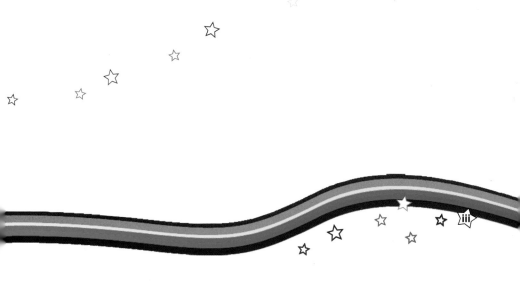

Until one has loved an animal
a part of one's soul remains unawakened.

— *Anatole France*

ACKNOWLEDGEMENTS

With my heartfelt love and gratitude, I thank my husband and best friend, Norman, for his unwavering faith, support and belief in me and my work for so many years. This book would not exist without him.

I would also like to thank my wonderful friends, colleagues, and fellow volunteers at the SPCA of Texas for their continued support and encouragement. In particular, I thank all those who have participated in and contributed to the Pet Grief Counseling Program. I have learned so very much from all of you.

In addition, I would like to thank my parents, Benjamin and Gerda Yapko, and my parents-in-law, Joe and Jean Pomerance, for their steadfast love, encouragement and support. I am also deeply grateful to my friends at K-9 Friends Visiting Therapy Dogs of GTDOG, as well as the Alaskan Malamute Assistance League and to Betty and Chris Christenson in particular. Those involved in animal rescue work are among the finest human beings I have ever known. It has truly been a privilege to be even a small part of this work.

And finally, and perhaps most importantly, I acknowledge the beauty, wisdom and spirit of all the wonderful animals who have brought such deep joy and meaning to my life. The dogs with whom I share my life now—Kianna, Tobias, Sedonia, Nenani, Kobuck, Sunny, Sophie, Chloe, Maximus, Hitchcock, Shadow and Emily—and those who have passed away but whose loving presence and guidance will forever bless and grace my life and the lives of others who have known and loved them—Lumberjack, Cinders, Bentley, Tasha, Jasper, Reggie, Agatha, Prince Rudolf the Third, Skookums, Alaska, Sugar Bear and Mariah. Each of you has taught me so very much.

Your pet is a very special friend . . .

one with whom you may work, study and play,

one with whom you may share joy and sorrow,

success and failure,

peace and understanding . . .

one with whom you may share

many happy, meaningful, memorable and magical moments,

a deep and powerful bond,

and a beautiful, true, and everlasting love.

 ust as our human companions come in many

different shapes, sizes, colors, and ages,

so do our animal friends appear in a vast array

of shapes, sizes, colors and ages.

Regardless of the differences in their appearance,

each may bring a unique gift of his or her own

and add great joy and meaning to your life.

Any animal with whom you share a special bond and
understanding, and with whom you feel comfortable
and at ease, may become your true and trusted friend.
A true friend loves and accepts you just as you are.
An animal companion may fill your life with joy, love,
faithfulness, devotion, and loyalty.
He may bring help, healing, and love to your heart.

Your companion communicates without words . . .
and has many ways of letting you know how he feels
and how much you are loved and respected by him.
He may seem to sense your needs and understand
what you are feeling deep in your heart.

ust like human beings, animal companions may serve many different and diverse purposes and play a wide variety of roles in life. For example, some dogs serve as seeing-eye dogs for the blind or act as ears for the hearing-impaired, or assist people with other types of disabilities. Some animals provide animal-assisted therapy; others assist police and firefighters in their work. Some provide water rescue and save people from drowning, while others help ranchers herd sheep or cattle. There are also animals (usually dogs) who help search for and rescue humans who have been affected by natural disasters such as floods, fires, tornadoes, volcanoes, hurricanes, earthquakes, and so on.

HOSPITAL

Your pet may seem to care about and share your feelings. She may provide comfort, or support you when you're sad, confused, frustrated, frightened or lonely.

Sleep Deprived in Seattle
WZZZ-TV

11

 erely by being with you and loving and accepting you, your pet may lighten your load. His presence may help put things in perspective and help you to view life's events with a receptive and open mind.

our animal companion may help reduce your stress,

fear, anger, depression, and anxiety, and may actually help

improve your health and overall well-being.

His presence may calm you down and help you to worry less.

Your friend may make you laugh when you really feel like crying.

He may teach you to "live in the moment" and to enjoy each

precious day instead of regretting things that may have

happened in the past or fearing things that may take place

in the future. His presence somehow seems to make the world

a more beautiful, harmonious, secure, and comfortable place.

atience, dignity, faithfulness, courage, and even gallantry may be taught to you by your animal companion. Through her example, you may learn to accept gracefully and humbly those events over which you have no control instead of complaining or whining.

No matter how difficult, frightening, or challenging your circumstances may be, your companion, just by being there for you, may encourage you to "KOKO" (Keep On Keeping On).

our animal companion may defend and protect you from harm or danger. In fact, she may even seem "angelic" and come to your rescue when you are in need of help. She will also keep your secrets, and never tell what you told her in confidence.

e may even save your life! Many people regard their pets as "angels" who have helped them cope with and recover from very sad, difficult, dangerous and trying times and circumstances. Their animals play a very important, unforgettable, and honorable role in their lives.

Along with all living creatures, you and your animal companion share our planet. Each of us plays an important role in surviving on, appreciating, taking care of, respecting, and preserving Mother Earth . . . not only for one another, but for future generations as well. Our interaction and mutual respect enable us to become increasingly aware of the purpose of our lives on earth and our interconnectedness and interdependence.

ou may learn a lot from your pet friend about love, loyalty

and devotion, for she offers her love and friendship uncondition-

ally without seeking reward, fame, success, or financial gain.

Nor does she care if you are rich, famous or powerful.

She is always on—and, if possible, by—your side . . .

no matter what. She may be your best friend, most trusted

confidante, advocate, champion, fellow adventurer and playmate.

And, she depends on your kindness.

hrough experiences with your animal companion,

you may learn many important lessons about life on Earth.

For example, through your animal companion, you may

learn about the miracle of birth and the gift of life itself.

ou may learn to value and accept all the experiences,

both joyful and sorrowful, that come your way as opportunities

to learn and grow, and to become stronger and wiser.

Through your relationship with him, you may also learn

much about gratitude and responsibility. You may learn to enjoy

and appreciate the world around you. You may also learn what it

feels like to have someone depend on you for food, water,

exercise and care.

You may also discover that you do not have to pretend

to be anything or anyone other than who you truly are

in order to be loved, for he loves you unconditionally . . .

and accepts, respects, and appreciates you just as you are.

our companion may serve as a guide who inspires you to follow your heart and your dreams, other than what others demand, suggest, or advise you to do.

Some of the happiest, most peaceful, beautiful, and memorable moments of your life may be experienced with your companion. Even when you least expect or anticipate them, your friend is there to share the beauty and significance of special times and events that you will remember and cherish forever.

It is wise to observe your companion's behavior and to respect and appreciate him for the unique being he is, for he, like you, is unlike any other living creature. Your relationship with him is precious and very special. He may bring to you some very special abilities, important lessons, and gifts that can deeply enrich your life.

And no matter how badly you behave or how many mistakes you may make, your animal companions do not hold a grudge. They forgive and love you anyway.

Although your animal companion may not speak with words or put thoughts and feelings into sentences, his heart somehow speaks to yours. There is a powerful bond and a sacred trust between you that can never be broken. And it is unlike any other bond.

Marshmallows

our pet is a true, loving, steadfast, and devoted friend who would, if he could, spend every precious moment of every day of your life with you. However, there will come the inevitable day when he must leave you—when he, like all human beings and all creatures on earth, will die.

However, he does not fear death. Rather, he quietly and peacefully accepts and embraces it as a part of life on earth, just as he accepts the change of the seasons . . .

the rebirth of life in spring,

the flowering and fruition of life in the summer,

the fading of life in the autumn, and

the seeming death of life in winter . . .

Or, the ebb and flow of the tides,

or the rising and setting of the sun.

hen your beloved pet dies, there will be a great void in your life and a deep ache in your heart that will never completely disappear. At the time of your animal's death, it is important to share your feelings of pain and sorrow with trusted friends, teachers, and family members. It is also a good idea to have a funeral or memorial service for your animal friend. It is also helpful to eulogize her . . . and to celebrate her life with friends who knew and loved her. You may wish to write a letter to her or a poem or a song or a story about her.

With the passage of time and the desire to remember and celebrate the beauty of your relationship and all that you have shared, you will eventually recover from your grief. And you will recognize and accept that loss is an inevitable part of the experience of life on Earth.

So do your very best to cherish and treasure each and

every moment you and your companion spend together.

For although there will be other wonderful animals in your life,

there will never be another quite like this one.

Hug him, hold him, pet him, tickle his belly, scratch behind his

ears, whisper to him and tell him how much you love him

and that you will never forget him.

Be sure to let him know how much he means to you,

and how grateful and appreciative you are for the time

you've had together. Regard your time together as a gift

and a privilege.

43

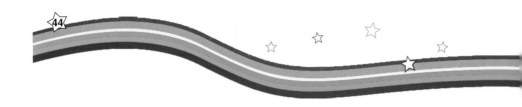

A bove all, remember that your beloved animal companion
has brought you many remarkable gifts . . . most importantly,
the greatest and most beautiful gift life has to offer
. . . the gift of LOVE.

Know that he is—and always will be—your true and loyal friend,
teacher, and guide. And that in your heart and mind, you will be
together joyously forever . . . and ever . . . and ever . . .

WORDS ABOUT OUR
ANIMAL COMPANIONS

An animal's eyes have the power
to speak a great language.

— *Martin Buber*

But ask now the beasts,
And they shall teach thee;
And the fowls of the air,
And they shall tell thee;
Or speak to the earth,
And it shall teach thee;
And the fishes of the sea
Shall declare unto thee.

— *Job 12:7-8 KJV*

A faithful friend is a strong protection.
A person who has found one has found a treasure.
A faithful friend is beyond price,
And his value cannot be weighed.
A faithful friend is a life-giving medicine.

— *The Apocrypha*

There is no wilderness like life without friends;
friendship multiplies blessings and minimizes misfortunes.
It is a unique remedy against adversity
and it soothes the soul.

— *Baltasar*

Not to hurt our humble brethren is our first duty to them,
but to stop there is not enough.
We have a higher mission— to be of service to them
whenever they require it.

— St. Francis of Assisi

Love all God's creation, the whole universe,
and each grain of sand. Love every leaflet,
every ray of God's light; love the beasts,
love the plants, love every creature.
When you love every creature,
you will understand the mystery of God
in created things.

— Fyodor Dostoevski

There is nothing of this earth more
proved than true friendship.

— *St. Thomas Aquinas*

Don't walk in front of me,
I may not follow.
Don't walk behind me,
I may not lead.
Walk beside me,
And just be my friend.

— *Anonymous*

If I spent enough time with the tiniest creature—even a
caterpillar—I would never have to prepare a sermon.
So full of God is every creature.

— *Meister Eckhart*

When I play with my cat, who knows if I am
not a pastime to her more than she is to me?

— *Montaigne*

Hear our prayer, Lord, for all animals.
May they be well-fed, well-treated, and happy.

— *Old Russian Prayer*

Our perfect companions never have fewer than four feet.

— *Colette*

Hear our humble prayer, O God, for our friends the animals. Especially for animals who are suffering; for any that are hunted or lost or deserted or frightened or hungry; for all that must be put to death. We entreat for them all Thy mercy and pity. And for those who deal with them we ask a heart of compassion and gentle hands, and kindly words. Make us true friends to animals and so to share the blessings of the merciful.

— *Albert Schweitzer*

The one absolutely unselfish friend that man can have
in this selfish world, the one that never deserts him,
the one that never proves ungrateful or treacherous,
is his dog. When all other friends desert, he remains.

— *George Graham Vest*

In a moonlit night, on a spring day,
The croak of a frog
Pierces the whole cosmos
And turns it into a single family!

— *Writings of Chang Chiu Ch'en*

Near this spot
Are deposited the remains of one
Who possessed beauty without vanity,
Strength without insolence,
Courage without ferocity,
And all the virtues of man without his vices . . .
This praise, which would be unmeaning flattery
If inscribed over human ashes,
Is but a just tribute to the memory of
Boatswain, a dog.

— *Lord Byron*

By ethical conduct toward all creatures
we enter a spiritual relationship with the universe.

— *Albert Schweitzer*

Hurt no living thing;
　　Ladybird, nor butterfly,
Nor moth with dusty wing,
　　Nor cricket chirping cheerily;
Nor grasshopper so light of leap,
　　Nor dancing gnat, nor beetle fat,
Nor harmless worms that creep.

— *Christina Rosetti*

What is man without the beasts?
If all the beasts were gone, men would die from great
loneliness of spirit, for whatever happens to the beasts also
happens to man. All things are connected. Whatever befalls
the earth befalls the children of the earth.

— *Chief Seattle*

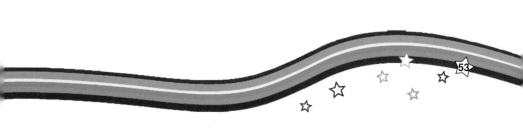

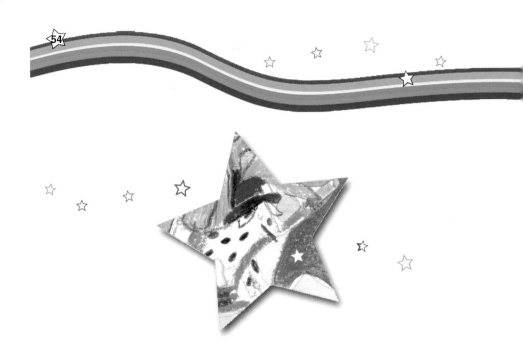

Animals are such agreeable friends . . .
They ask no questions,
They pass no criticisms.

— *George Eliot*

The greatness of a nation and its moral progress
can be judged by the way its animals are treated.

— *Mohandas Ghandi*

We need another and wiser and perhaps more mystical concept of animals. We patronize them for their incompleteness, for their tragic fate of having taken form so far below ourselves. And therein we err, we greatly err. For the animal shall not be measured by man. In a world older and more complete than ours they move finished and complete, gifted with extensions of the senses we have lost or never attained, living by voices we shall never hear. They are not brethren, they are not underlings. They are other nations, caught with ourselves in the net of life and time, fellow prisoners of the splendour and the travail ahead.

— *Henry Beston*

Any religion not based on respect for life
is not a true religion. Until he extends his
circle of compassion to all living things,
man will not himself find peace.

— *Albert Schweitzer*

I would give nothing for that man's religion
Whose very dog and cat are not the better for it!

— *Rowland Hill*

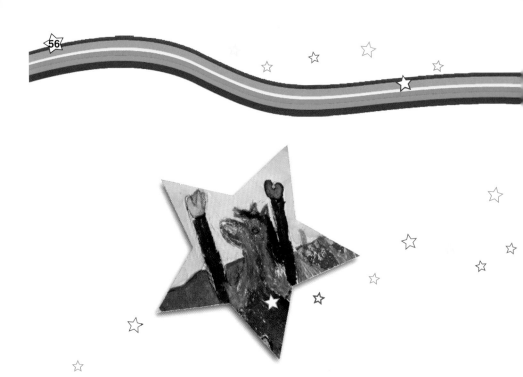

We are part of the earth and it is part of us.
The perfumed flowers are our sisters; the deer, the horse,
the great eagle, these are our brothers. The rocky crests,
the juices of the meadows, the body heat of the pony,
and man — all belong to the same family.

— *Chief Seattle*

There must be a heaven for the animal friends we love.
They are not human, yet they bring out our own humanity . . .
Sometimes in ways that other people cannot.
They do not worry about fame or fortune . . .
Instead, they bring our hearts nearer
to the joy of simple things.
Each day they teach us little lessons
in trust and steadfast affection.
Whatever heaven may be, there's surely a place in it
for friends as good as these.

— *Author Unknown*

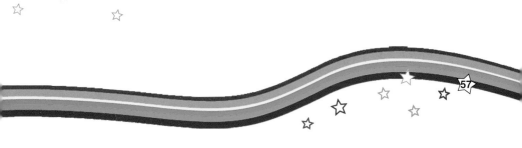

ABOUT THE AUTHOR

DIANE POMERANCE received her Ph.D. in Communications from the University of Michigan, Ann Arbor. She has been certified as a **Grief Recovery Specialist** by the internationally recognized Grief Recovery Institute. She was trained directly by the founder of the Institute, John W. James.

Dr. Pomerance counsels those grieving from any loss; however, she has a special interest in those mourning the loss of a beloved companion animal. The loss of a pet can be devastating to adults as well as children.

Dr. Pomerance created, established, and serves as director of the Pet Grief Counseling Program for the SPCA of Texas. In addition to serving as an active volunteer for the **SPCA of Texas,** she is also an active member of **K-9 Friends Visiting Dogs of GTDOG**, and the **Alaskan Malamute Assistance League**. She is the author of numerous articles and the highly acclaimed children's book, *When Your Pet Dies.* She lives in North Texas with her husband and twelve canine "kids."

ABOUT THE ILLUSTRATOR

VANESSA MIER attends Haltom High School in the Dallas/Fort Worth, Texas area. She has received numerous awards and accolades for her artistic work. She illustrated a children's book on pet loss called *When Your Pet Dies.*

Animal Companions represents her second professional experience as an artist.

☆ (So that you don't have to damage your book,
permission to photocopy this form is granted.)

ORDER FORM

We hope you enjoyed this book from **Polaire Publications.**
If you would like to order additional copies, please complete
this form and send with payment to:

POLAIRE PUBLICATIONS ☆
PMB 217
2221 Justin Rd., Ste. 219
☆ **Flower Mound, Texas 75028**
or you may fax your order to: **(972) 691-9134**
or visit **www.animalcompanionsandtheirpeople.com**

Name _____

Address _____

City, State, Zip _____

_____ No. books ordered x **$9.95**   = $ _____
Shipping & Handling: **$3.50**
for first book, plus **$1.00**
for each additional book   = $ _____
Subtotal   = $ _____
(Texas residents,
please add 7.25% sales tax)   = $ _____
TOTAL   = $ _____

☐ Check: Please make payable to **Polaire Publications**.
☐ Credit Card:
    ☐ MasterCard   ☐ Visa

Card # _____

Exp. Date _____

Signature_____

$1 of each copy of this book sold will be donated to: